Life After Loss

Hannah Cowan

BookLeaf Publishing

India | USA | UK

Life After Loss © 2023 Hannah Cowan

All rights reserved.

No part of this publication may be reproduced, stored in a retrieval system, or transmitted, in any form or by any means, electronic, mechanical, photocopying, recording or otherwise, without the prior written permission of the presenters.

Hannah Cowan asserts the moral right to be identified as author of this work.

Presentation by *BookLeaf Publishing*

Web: www.bookleafpub.com

E-mail: info@bookleafpub.com

ISBN: 9789358738063

First edition 2023

*To my dad, Alan for always pushing me to make
my dreams come true.*

ACKNOWLEDGEMENT

Thank you to my mum and dad for all life's lessons you have taught me over the years and the guidance you have given me. Thank you to my wonderful husband for believing in me and giving me the confidence to take this leap.

PREFACE

In the days following the death of my dad, I found comfort in writing down my feelings and reading other poems and sayings about loss. Both my dad and I wished to write a book so publishing the poems I have written fulfils not only my dream but his too.

Grief My Dear

Grief my dear
Is always near
It's just around the corner

Unseen unheard
And quite absurd
You won't know how you'll feel

Tears of sorrow
May change tomorrow
Or anger may seep through

Whilst it will not go
In time I know
You grief is sure to ease

Tears

They're hot on your face
And salty to taste
A little one escapes
Or a thousand fall
Dampening your skin
Making tracks on your cheeks
They may come once a day
And sometimes more often
But one thing we know
Our tears always flow

A View From A Window

A view from a window
Clouds floating in the breeze
The sunshine peeping through
And lighting up the trees

A flock of birds fly high
Soaring in the distance
Sheep graze in the field
I dream of your existence

You're out there somewhere
A new journey has begun
Please don't forget us
But be sure to have some fun

Grief

Gone from our touch not from our hearts
Rolling tears stream on and on
In time the pain will slowly fade
Ease away but not forgotten
Forever in our thoughts and memories

Harbour

5

As the waves danced on the darkened shore
The stars shone bright like never before
The ships in the harbour, masts standing tall
Began to rattle, a metal clinking squall

However all was calm at the break of dawn
The people rose with a stretch and a yawn
A new day was starting, the sun in the sky
The birds hopping round, the world going by

The day went on, passing by in a blur
The sea on the shore a soft sounding purr
The light was fading and dusk setting in
A slither of moon looking ever so thin

As night fell again, another day done
Our lives continuing without you, our one
We think of you daily though you're gone from our touch
Your memory lives on, we love you so much

We'll Meet Again

As we walked along a stony beach
With pebbles big and small
It gave us space and time to think
Where are you after all?

There should be four of us not three
It doesn't feel the same
We wish you were right here with us
Although you're not to blame

You're in a better place right now
Free of all the hurt and pain
We will be strong as life goes on
One day we'll meet again

Life's Path

When life is hanging by a thread
Don't leave your words left unsaid
Our futures are not guaranteed
No one knows where they will lead

Your path may change along the way
We are not promised each new day
So make each one feel sublime
As there is no telling of our time

Without You

Does grief last forever
Or does time really heal
I wonder if he knows
Just how we all feel

One minute you're fine
The next you are not
Living without you
Is going to pot

You were the strong one
The light of our life
Whatever we do
Our feelings are rife

Is that you we see
Up there in the sky
With the birds and the bees
Flying so high

You may have gone
Moved on somewhere new
But please don't forget
We will always love you

What Do I Do

I sit
I stare
Into the air

I think
I wait
Full of hate

I bawl
I cry
Watch the world go by

I long
I love
For you above

Weatherman

A passing shower
A fleeting storm
I'm glad I'm here
In the warm

The rain it falls
The wind it blows
I hide inside
Until it goes

The sun comes out
The sky so bright
Along you go
Into the light

The moon it shines
The planets glow
You have gone
But this we know

In the heavens
Amongst the stars
You look down
From yours to ours

Tower In The Sky

We have not cried
We are so numb
In this new life
We will succumb

It's all consuming
Day by day
One day soon
We'll find our way

A new chapter
Has now begun
But without you
Your time is done

We think of you
Each waking hour
As you shine upon us
From your sky tower

My Body

Tears stream down my face
They come and they go
Just like a winding river
They ebb and they flow

My heart feels so empty
It beats with an ache
Just like all the silence
It keeps me awake

The air in my chest
Is rattling around
Just like a trapped animal
Is begging to be found

This feeling is paralysing
All my energy has gone
Just like a bee sting
All the hurt does go on

My body it knows
You are not coming back
Just like a lost bird
You are on a new track

Somewhere

Over the rainbow
You fly so high
Under the rainbow
Our days pass by

Above the sky
You look down
Below the sky
We slowly drown

Out at sea
You float around
On the shore
We are ground

Within the stars
You shine so bright
Back down on earth
Our guiding light

Wherever I Go

Wherever I go
I hope you will follow
Whether high up a mountain
Or down in a hollow

Wherever I go
I hope you're with me
We can visit new places
Catch some sun by the sea

Wherever I go
I hope you are near
So you guide us through life
And ease all our fear

Wherever I go
I hope will see
Your guidance in life
Really shaped me

Dark Nights

As I lie in a darkened room
Trying to drift off to sleep
The memories are flooding back
Into my pillow I start to weep

I still can't quite believe you're gone
That I'll never lay eyes on you
All that's left is the mark you made
On the good times and bad too

I know you're somewhere looking down
And will be with me all the way
I will be strong and live my life
Until we meet again one day

I'm Fine

How are you? I'm fine thank you
The easiest words to say
When in reality deep inside
You crumble alone each day

How are you? I'm fine thank you
We lie to make others at ease
When in reality all we want to do
Is give those lost a squeeze

How are you? I'm fine thank you
Some days we are just that
When in reality we are staying strong
We live we laugh we chat

How are you? Im fine thank you
You answer without a thought
When in reality we are actually good
Time heals the battles we've fought

The Long And Winding Road

The long and winding road
Goes ever on and on
To a place you once lived
From which you are now gone

The sun shines through the trees
The wildlife plays in the road
A view that stretches for miles
And sheep by the bucket load

The long and winding road
Goes ever round and round
Along to a small village
Is where you can be found

The sun shines in the sky above
The birds they dance and soar
You are again at home to rest
And live here forever more

Our Time

Time waits for nobody
The clock hands do tick by
So live your life to the max
And go out on a high

We all will have our time one day
To take our final stroll
When we're old and tired
And life has taken its toll

The time we have is precious
Make the most of all you do
And know that one day again
I will be back with you

Home Again

Do you know
Where I will go
When I am at the end

A sunny place
An open space
Is where I will reside

Please visit me
Come and see
The place I do now rest

A lovely view
Close to you
Finally home again

Funny Man

As I sit and think of you
A few words come to mind
Funny, witty and unique
But most of all so kind

You really were a treasure
So very special to the end
Even if throughout your years
You drove us round the bend

You loved a joke and laugh
Made up silly ditties too
A chuckle a day you would say
You cannot have too few

I am my fathers daughter
Here to carry on your quick wit
And continue making people laugh
If not, I'll have to quit!

If This Is Goodbye

A battle you have fought so strong
We hope you are at ease
In our hearts you will belong
Just don't forget us please

We will learn to live without you
Each passing day is hard
With all that we have been through
We are forever scarred

It's time to say goodbye today
And lay you down to rest
We're sure you'll find your way
Up there to party with the best

We hope we've done you proud
A day for us all to remember
To pay respects and talk aloud
Since your death back in September